THAT'S A JOB?

I like
HELPING PEOPLE

... what jobs
are there?

by Amanda Learmonth
Illustrated by Elise Gaignet

Kane Miller
A DIVISION OF EDC PUBLISHING

CONTENTS

Nurse 26

Midwife 27

Occupational therapist 28

Postal worker 30

Medical research scientist 32

School counselor 34

Human resources manager 35

911 Dispatcher 36

Paramedic 37

Lawyer 38

Pharmacist 40

Dentist 41

Firefighter 42

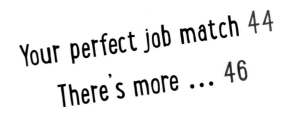

INTRODUCTION

Qualities and skills needed for jobs that involve helping others

There are lots of jobs you can do to help people, some of which you may not even know about.

Are you someone who helps people when they're in trouble? Do you have a big heart and a sense of fairness? If so, a career focused on helping people might be just right for you.

From working in science and medicine to education and the emergency services, there are many jobs out there for those who want to help people.

Each job needs different people with different skills: doctors, nurses, and paramedics need excellent medical knowledge, lawyers and politicians need confident speaking skills, while firefighters and dispatchers need to be able to stay calm under pressure.

But there are some qualities that everyone who works with people should have: a kind, caring nature, and a desire to make a difference to others' lives, whether by easing someone's pain, fixing their car, or finding new cures for diseases.

Quite often you'll need courage and stamina: you may have to work long hours, sometimes through the night, and you may face danger in order to save or protect your community. Many jobs require a love of learning, as well. For instance, scientists, pharmacists, and psychologists spend many years studying and training before they can start working.

Whatever the job, you'll need a passion for helping your community. Whether you're in a school, a hospital, an office, or a laboratory, doing your best to improve the lives of other people will be really important to you.

If this sounds like you, then you're the right type of person for a job helping people!

This book looks at 25 different jobs that give you a sneak peek into a typical day in the life of each worker. You'll learn the important stuff, such as what it takes to get the job and what duties and tasks are involved, and you'll discover the fun stuff, too, such as the worst part of a postal worker's job ...

HINT: It involves overexcited pets!

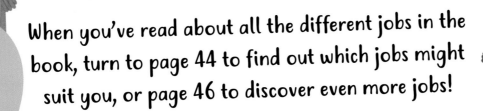

When you've read about all the different jobs in the book, turn to page 44 to find out which jobs might suit you, or page 46 to discover even more jobs!

SPECIAL EDUCATION TEACHER

My sister has learning difficulties, and I grew up wanting to help children like her who find it harder to learn than others. I went to college to become a special education teacher, and now I work at a local elementary school. It's my job to help children with learning difficulties, including intellectual and physical disabilities, achieve their very best—and enjoy their education, too!

I spend most of my time working alongside classroom teachers, focusing on helping the students with learning difficulties. Other times I work one-on-one or in small groups outside of the classroom. In some schools, special education teachers have self-contained classrooms.

1

It's 6:00 a.m., and my alarm goes off. As a teacher, my day starts early! I need plenty of time to get ready for the busy day ahead.

2x4	5x4
3x4	6x4
4x4	7x4

2

At 8:00 a.m., I arrive at school. Classes don't start for another hour, so I use the time to check my schedule for the day and make sure I have all my lesson plans ready. I always write these lesson plans in advance. It's important to be very organized in this job!

3

First period is math. I'll be working with a small group of students while the classroom teacher teaches the rest of the class. It's good to set a happy and positive tone, so as the children arrive, I say hello and give them each a big smile. I then make sure they are all calmly settled in their seats and ready to start learning.

4

I can see that one of my students is struggling and is starting to get really frustrated. We count to ten while he breathes slowly. He soon calms down and the rest of the lesson goes smoothly. I often use strategies like this to help students manage their emotions, and always try to stay patient and calm myself.

5

After recess, it's time for reading. I'm working one-on-one with a student who wasn't able to read at the beginning of the year. This student is on the autism spectrum and can be sensitive to lots of noise, so we work in a quiet room. I listen as she reads aloud, then give her a big thumbs-up. I feel proud that she's made such great progress!

6

After lunch, I head to a meeting with a speech and language therapist (see page 46). We discuss one of the children who has difficulties with speaking. He gives me some ideas to improve the student's speaking skills, such as using signs and pictures to help them remember words. I often work with experts like this, including reading specialists and educational psychologists.

7

Next up, it's gym class. They're playing basketball, and I take time to watch one of my students who uses a wheelchair. It's great to see her having so much fun!

8

Soon it's home time for the students, but not for me! I stay a little longer to review tomorrow's lessons, grade work, and write up reports. Before I head home, I check my mailbox, and there's a card from a student who recently graduated, thanking me for supporting them—what a lovely end to the day!

THANK YOU!

MY JOB: BEST AND WORST PARTS

BEST: I love the variety; from the different kids to the different subjects, every day is unique.

WORST: Making sure my students get equal time and attention can be hard sometimes, but I try my best.

SOCIAL WORKER

Social workers help people to deal with problems they face in their everyday lives. I'm a foster care social worker. I help children who need a temporary caregiver to find a foster home—a safe, loving place to stay until they can return home or find a new family to live with. I work closely with the children and foster families to make sure everyone is happy and getting along well.

After earning a master's degree in social work, I got a job at a foster care agency. I chose to specialize in families and children, but other social workers work with people with disabilities, the elderly, or those with mental health problems. We all have one thing in common, and that's a passion for helping people in need to lead safe, happy lives.

1

It's Monday morning and I'm at the agency, checking emails and making plans for the week ahead. I've been assigned a new foster family to work with— they recently passed our agency checks and training program, and are now licensed. It's great news—we always need more foster families! They're approved to foster multiple children, and we have twin siblings who need a temporary home, so I give them a call to arrange the next steps.

2

Next, I head out for my first visit of the day: to a foster parent who has recently taken in a young boy. I catch up with the boy first, and I'm pleased to find that he is settling in. The parent is concerned he's not eating well enough though, since he's very unsure of new foods. I give her some ideas to try, such as introducing one new food at a time. I reassure her that she is doing a really great job, and that I'll visit them again in a month.

3

I return to the agency to write a report of my visit, and for a meeting with my team. We are organizing an information fair for next week, for people interested in becoming foster parents. Our marketing manager has prepared flyers and posters to advertise the event. We hope lots of people will come!

4

After lunch, it's time to lead a training session for new foster parents. In these sessions, the foster parents learn how to give children the best possible care. Last time we went over parenting skills, and tips on managing misbehavior. Today, we have hired a trainer to teach basic first aid.

5

In the afternoon I have another home visit, this time to check on a little girl who has recently been adopted. Sometimes, children move on from foster care because they have been adopted by a new family. I'm here to make sure everything is going well. We talk, and it's clear she is healthy, happy, and thriving—she even shows me a drawing she has done of her adopted family!

6

It's 5:00 p.m. and time for something I've been really looking forward to: our achievement award ceremony! We love to encourage and recognize the achievements of young people in our care, and tonight we're holding a costume party at our local community center. I quickly get changed into my costume and drive over to the party.

MY JOB: BEST AND WORST PARTS

BEST: I love helping children who have had a difficult time to find a safe, happy home.

WORST: There is a lot of paperwork—forms to fill in and reports to write. But it's an important part of the job so I know it has to be done!

7

The party is in full swing, with games, music, and a magician, too. The children love receiving their "Superstar" certificates for achievements like being brave, trying hard, and helping others. It's a fantastic end to my day!

DOCTOR

In my job as a family doctor, every day is different! When someone is injured or feeling unwell, I'm usually the first person they will come to see. A primary care physician treats all kinds of conditions, from minor aches and pains to more serious ailments. I see patients of all ages, some whom I've known since they were tiny babies!

It takes many years of study to become a doctor. After studying biology in college, I went to medical school for four years. I then did a residency at different hospitals and health centers before joining a practice. Some doctors choose to specialize in other areas of medicine such as pediatrics (children's health), surgery (performing operations), or psychiatry (mental health).

3

Next, I see a patient for a follow-up appointment. When I saw him a few weeks ago, his blood pressure was very high, which could lead to serious health issues. I advised him to exercise more, and to eat a healthier diet with fewer salty and fatty foods. I'm so pleased to find that he has lost some weight and his blood pressure has gone down. Encouraging people to lead a healthy lifestyle is often a big part of my job.

2

At 8:00 a.m., my first appointment begins—I'm checking the health of a newborn baby. I measure the baby's weight and height, then record the measurements on his chart. Everything looks great; he's growing really well! Before I say goodbye, I make sure to remind his mother to schedule an appointment for his immunizations (injections to prevent diseases).

1

I arrive at the practice around 7:30 a.m., which gives me just enough time to greet the receptionist, change into my white coat, and look at my schedule. I have appointments all through the day— it's going to be busy!

4

An elderly woman is my next appointment. She has had a rash on her arms for several weeks, and it's not getting any better. I refer her to a dermatologist—a doctor who specializes in skin diseases—so she can make an appointment. I'm not always able to diagnose or treat particular conditions, such as skin diseases, so in these cases, I refer my patients to specialist doctors.

5

I finish the morning writing notes in my patients' medical records. It's important to keep these current so I can check patients' progress and keep track of any medication they are taking. I also take time to answer emails and write referrals. Good computer skills are essential in my work.

6

My next patient is struggling to sleep and suffering feelings of anxiety. As she talks, the patient becomes more upset and begins to have a panic attack—she feels nauseous and struggles to breathe. I explain what's happening and reassure her. I ask her to watch as I move my arm up and down slowly—techniques like this help to distract and calm. After a few minutes, the attack ends. I then spend time talking to the patient about ways to improve her sleep, techniques to help her anxiety, and I suggest she make an appointment with a mental health counselor.

7

I have one more patient to see: a teenager who broke his leg in a skiing accident a few weeks ago. I check his latest X-ray and can see that the bone is healing well, so I arrange for him to see a physical therapist (see page 47) who will help him to build back the strength in his leg.

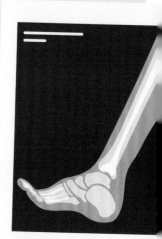

MY JOB: BEST AND WORST PARTS

BEST: I really enjoy building a strong, trusting relationship with my patients.

WORST: It can be very hard to give patients bad news about their health.

8

It's almost the end of the day—I write prescriptions, type up more notes, and spend an hour reading medical articles, to keep my knowledge up-to-date. I'm ready to go home and relax, but not before I go for a run—I have to make sure to take care of my own health, too!

POLICE OFFICER

As a police officer, it's my duty to protect my community and help prevent crime. Every day, I drive around the city streets in my patrol car, looking out for anyone who is not following the law, and helping out in emergencies. I never know what's going to happen from one day to the next, and that's one reason why I love my job!

I joined the police academy after high school. I then spent six months studying, training, and learning practical skills such as first aid—and how to safely drive vehicles at high speed!

1

I arrive at the police station in time for a team briefing with the sergeant. She tells us which part of the city we'll each be patrolling on our shifts today.

2

My partner and I head out to our patrol car. We always work together—luckily we get along really well! We check all our equipment and make sure everything is in working order, switch on our police radio, and we're ready for duty ...

3

It doesn't take long before we get our first call. There's been a vehicle crash. We don't know yet how serious it is, so we need to get there as quickly as we can, to make sure no one is in danger. Time to activate the lights and siren!

4

We arrive at the scene of the crash. A car and a truck have collided. Luckily, no one is hurt. My partner tapes off the scene and redirects traffic, while I talk to the drivers. I take their statements and write everything down—an important part of my job is taking statements and writing reports. The tow trucks soon arrive to clear away the damaged vehicles, and we go back on patrol.

5

Next, we are called to a possible burglary. The homeowner had returned from the store, heard strange noises in the house, and wisely decided to wait outside and call 911. My partner and I carefully search the home. We find the intruder, but it's not a person breaking the law—it's a friendly dog who belongs to one of the neighbors! Once we're sure all is safe, we advise the homeowner to close the windows when they go out in the future, and we return the mischievous dog to its home.

6

Back on patrol, we notice a car going really fast—it's breaking the speed limit. We signal for the car to pull over, and I issue the driver a ticket and explain that he will have to pay a fine. At first, he is angry, but then he apologizes. Patience and good communication skills always come in handy in situations like this.

7

Our shift is almost over and we're about to head back to the station. Suddenly, a woman runs over in a panic. She has lost her little girl on the crowded sidewalk. My partner and I quickly split up to search for her. Thankfully, I find her, peering through a store window. Mom and daughter are happily reunited—it's moments like this that remind me why I love my job!

MY JOB: BEST AND WORST PARTS

BEST: Knowing that I help to keep my community safe is the proudest feeling. I also enjoy having a partner to support and rely on.

WORST: Some cases can be upsetting, especially when innocent people are hurt or distressed.

DAYCARE CENTER MANAGER

I always loved babysitting when I was younger, so I knew I wanted to work with children. After high school, I took classes at a community college, then I started as a daycare assistant before I worked my way up to manager. Now, I'm in charge of running a daycare center, where we look after young children while their parents are at work. There's never a boring moment—every day is busy, loud, and fun!

The most important thing to have in this job is a passion for working with children. It also helps to be patient, cheerful, and have lots of energy!

1

It's 7:30 a.m., and time for a quick meeting with the daycare staff about today's tasks before the children arrive. The daycare center has different rooms for each age group: babies, toddlers, and preschoolers. We start by preparing the preschool room, putting out lots of paints, crayons, and play dough in the art area.

2

At 8:00 a.m., we greet the children with big smiles as they arrive, and help them hang up their coats. One child is a little upset after saying goodbye to her mom—it happens sometimes. I think I have something that will cheer her up: painting! I show her the art table and soon enough she is happily painting with her friends.

3

I walk around each room, checking that the staff are watching the children and writing notes. The notes are really important for keeping the parents up-to-date with what their child has been doing all day. Most of the children are still too young to be able to tell their parents what kind of a day they've had!

4

I spend the rest of the morning in my office. As a manager, my time is split between helping with the children and doing office work. I answer emails, update paperwork, order new art supplies, and arrange tours for parents who are interested in visiting the daycare center.

5

Next, I visit the babies' room. I run a safety check to make sure there are no small objects the babies might choke on. Then it's time for water play with some of the toddlers. Now I remember why I always bring a change of clothes!

6

At lunchtime, I help the staff get the children fed. Each child has their own care plan. This tells us about their medical needs or allergies, to keep them safe and healthy. One little boy is diabetic, so I make sure he receives his medication. I've had special training to administer medications, so I know what to do.

7

I help clean up, then it's "quiet time," when most children take a nap. After their rest, the children go outside to play. Meanwhile, I meet some parents who are thinking about enrolling their child here. I give them a tour of the center. They seem really impressed and would like to sign up right away.

8

It's 6:00 p.m., and I can't believe it's the end of the day already. The parents arrive to collect their children. We show each parent their child's notes, and say goodbye. There's just time to tidy up before heading home for some quiet time of my own!

MY JOB: BEST AND WORST PARTS

BEST: I love seeing the children learn new skills. And there's always something to giggle about!

WORST: When children leave the center to start school, or if their families move away, it can be sad to say goodbye.

REFUSE COLLECTOR

Most people don't think about what happens to their garbage once they've put it out on the street. That's where I come in! As a refuse collector for the city, I drive around the neighborhood, emptying garbage cans from outside people's homes. It may not seem very glamorous, but I'm proud to help keep our streets clean and garbage free!

After high school I took a training course to learn how to operate garbage trucks. I then learned the routes, health and safety rules, and day-to-day tasks on the job. These days, I often help new colleagues learn the ropes.

1
It's 5:00 a.m., and the sun isn't up, but I'm already at the sanitation yard where the garbage trucks are parked. My job always starts early, so it's lucky I'm a morning person! Before I set out on my eight-hour shift, I check my truck for any problems and fill the tires with air. I'm ready to go!

2
I drive a different route every day and stay in touch with colleagues using a radio. I barely need to leave the truck! I use the automated arm on my truck to pick up the garbage cans. It reaches out to grab the can and pours the trash into a container on the truck. The garbage is then crushed to make room for more.

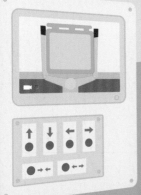

3
Inside the cab, there are controls for moving the automated arm and a monitor to show me what's going on outside. It's a bit like playing a video game!

4
By 8:00 a.m., I have already picked up 250 cans. Only 550 more to go! I wave to some children who have come out to watch. I remember doing the same thing when I was their age. I was crazy about trucks, too!

5
After my shift, I drive to the landfill. This is where the garbage is dumped and later buried. Finally, I return the truck to the yard then walk home—after all that sitting, it's nice to stretch my legs!

MY JOB: BEST AND WORST PARTS

BEST: I love that I'm serving my community.

WORST: On windy days, cans often get blown over and I have to pick up the mess.

SHIPPING CLERK

Have you ever wondered how the things you need end up in stores? That's where shipping clerks come in! We make sure goods get from place to place. I work in a commercial bakery as a shipping clerk. My job is to see that the loaves of bread we bake are packed correctly and delivered on time to stores across the region, fresh and ready for people to buy.

I needed a job right after high school, so I was really glad to start working at the bakery. I'm learning on the job: one day, with experience and hard work, I hope to become a supervisor.

1

As soon as I arrive at work, I print the report for today's orders. It shows me how many trays of bread need to be shipped to customers, and the addresses where they need to go. Most of the day I'm on my feet, but good computer skills are also important, since I'm often checking reports, keeping records, and printing mailing labels.

2

Next, I head to the packaging department where the loaves are ready to be shipped. I inspect each loaf for damage—nobody likes squished bread! I also check that the number of loaves in each tray matches each order on my report. I have to be good at spotting mistakes.

3

Once the orders are ready, it's time for my favorite part of the job: driving the forklift! I load the trays, drive them over to the delivery truck, then carefully unload them.

4

Once all the orders are packed on the truck, the delivery driver takes over. Next stop, the grocery store, then someone's plate for lunch!

MY JOB: BEST AND WORST PARTS

BEST: I like knowing that I'm helping people get their toast for breakfast!

WORST: All the lifting and carrying can be hard work, but it keeps me fit.

17

DEVELOPMENT DIRECTOR

I've always enjoyed raising money for charity, whether it was selling lemonade in the front yard or washing cars for my neighbors. Now it's my job! I'm in charge of raising money for a charity that helps elderly people. Some elderly people are lonely or no longer able to care for themselves. My charity helps in many ways, from organizing volunteer visits to keep people company, to teaching computer skills so they can keep in touch with loved ones.

1

It's early morning and, on my way to the office, I stop at a local elementary school to pick up a check. The school recently held a fun run, where the staff and students took part, and raised money for our charity. They managed to raise $500! I make sure to snap a photo for our website, and I thank the school for all their efforts.

$500.00

I studied marketing and fundraising management in college. I learned how to give presentations, arrange events, manage teams of people, and look after the money side of things. It helps to be really creative, too, since I have to come up with new fundraising ideas!

2

At the office, I check my messages. There's one from someone who wants to join our charity as a volunteer. I give them a call and invite them to attend an orientation day next month— these days are set up to train new volunteers. I'm thankful for all our volunteers because they help in so many ways, from the running of events to spreading awareness of what our charity does.

3

Next, it's time for a meeting with my team. We share some ideas for future fundraising events: a charity golf day, a quiz night, a book sale. Then we talk about our big yearly event—the summer garden party. It's happening later today, and I'm really excited. It's our chance to raise a lot of money!

4

I spend the rest of the morning writing letters and emails to encourage people to donate to our charity. I receive an email from a grandfather who has just finished a sponsored bicycle ride. He's raised over $1,000. What a star! I share his story on our website, and I make sure to send him a thank-you letter in reply.

5

Over lunch, I meet with the owner of a bakery. She is interested in donating cupcakes for our fundraising events. In return, we will advertise her company in our newsletter, on our website, and on social media. It's a great partnership.

6

It's time for the party! Our volunteers have set everything up, and the guests start arriving—it's great to see so many people from the community here. We have a number of stands selling donated items, from food to clothing, including colorful scarfs knitted by some of the elderly people the charity has been helping. I welcome the guests, and make sure everything is running smoothly.

7

The party is a huge success! I give a speech to thank everyone for coming, and to remind them that the money they have spent will go back to helping the charity carry on all its good work.

8

Once the guests have left, I help clean up, then it's time to go home. Tomorrow, we'll find out how much money we raised. As a reward for a successful day, I treat myself to one of the cupcakes from earlier—delicious!

MY JOB: BEST AND WORST PARTS

BEST: I'm always on the go, which I love! And making a difference in people's lives is really rewarding, too.

WORST: Cleaning up after a fundraising event is no one's favorite job!

PSYCHOLOGIST

Why do we think and behave in the way that we do? What's going on inside our brains? These questions have always fascinated me, and that's why I became a psychologist! After earning a PhD in psychology and doing lots of work experience, I earned my license, and now I work as a clinical psychologist. I enjoy helping people with mental illnesses to understand their problems, find ways to cope, and change their lives for the better.

As a clinical psychologist, I work in a private practice, where I meet patients individually or in groups. Some psychologists treat people in hospitals, mental health centers, schools, or colleges. Others work as researchers or professors at universities, studying the human mind and behavior in detail.

1
I start my day with yoga and breathing exercises. This helps keep me calm and prepares me for the day ahead. I have to make sure I look after my own physical and mental health, or I won't be much help to anyone else!

2
At 8:30 a.m., I get to work and go straight to my office. I check through my schedule and make sure I have my patients' notes ready. I will be seeing some regular patients today, and some new patients, too.

3
My first session is with a family I've been seeing for a few weeks. Their teenage son was refusing to listen or talk to his parents. Over the past few sessions, I've been trying to encourage them to work together as a team, and to listen to each other. Today, we had a really good discussion, and no one got angry or upset. I think we are making progress!

4

My next appointment is with a young woman who suffers from anxiety and panic attacks. She feels like the techniques she usually uses aren't enough anymore. After giving her time to talk through her concerns, I suggest she try some light exercise, like going for a walk, every day. Exercise has lots of benefits, including helping with sleep and mood, and often helps distract people from negative thoughts. She's keen to try it, so I write down our ideas in her treatment plan.

5

Next, a new patient comes to see me. Since this is his first visit, I begin by asking him some questions to encourage him to talk. Then I ask him to complete a personality test. This will help me get to know him better. It's just the start: with new clients, it can take many sessions to build their trust and understand their difficulties.

6

It's almost lunchtime. I just have time to write up my patients' notes before a meeting. This is my chance to get advice and discuss ideas with our practice head, a very experienced psychologist. Talking things through helps me to think of different ways I can work with my patients.

7

In the afternoon, I lead a group therapy session for people suffering from depression. For some patients, group sessions give them a chance to talk to other people who are experiencing some of the same feelings. With my encouragement, the participants share their stories and problems. It's rewarding to see them helping each other.

8

It's the end of the day, so I finish writing up my notes and head home to my two dogs. They're always ready to help me relax and unwind after a long day!

MY JOB: BEST AND WORST PARTS

BEST: I love using my skills to help people make positive changes.

WORST: It can be difficult to see people so troubled or unhappy.

BUS DRIVER

I loved riding the bus when I was a kid, and I'd often pretend to be the driver. Today, I do it for real! I drive passengers around the city, making sure they arrive on time and safely. I had to complete a training program, pass physical, hearing, and vision tests, and and earn a special license to get my job. It makes me happy to know that I'm taking people where they want to go!

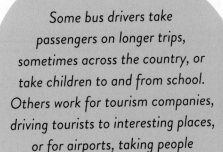

Some bus drivers take passengers on longer trips, sometimes across the country, or take children to and from school. Others work for tourism companies, driving tourists to interesting places, or for airports, taking people to and from their cars.

1
Today I'm up early. I arrive at the bus depot at 5:00 a.m., where I check which route I will be driving before I head to my assigned bus. I'll spend my shift driving the same route over and over, but I won't be bored—I love to drive, plus there's always plenty to see and lots of people to meet. Off I go!

2
It's still dark, but I know the route really well. I check for waiting passengers at each stop and greet them with a smile as they climb on board. Being friendly and good with people is important in this job. Knowing the city is also important because I often advise lost passengers on which routes to take.

3
On my break, I get a call from the depot. Uh-oh ... a passenger thinks they left something on my bus—their child's favorite toy! I check the bus and soon find it. Phew! At the end of my shift, I'll leave it at the depot so the passenger can come and collect it.

4
As the day goes on, I stop to pick up more people, including an elderly man called Charlie. He's a regular, who takes the bus downtown every day, to shop, socialize, and get out of the house. I help him onto the bus with his groceries. Knowing I can help people get around is one of the best parts of my job.

5
It's the end of my shift, so I drive the bus back to the depot where another driver will take over my route. I wonder what tomorrow will bring!

MY JOB: BEST AND WORST PARTS

BEST: Meeting lots of different people every day is great!

WORST: Sitting for long periods of time can be a bit uncomfortable.

MECHANIC

I like working with my hands: I'm always taking things apart and fixing them! I'm also passionate about cars, and that's why I chose to be a mechanic. After high school, I got a diploma from a technical school, then spent time learning on the job. Now I work in a large repair shop. Cars are an important part of many people's lives, and I make sure they stay safe on the road.

Some mechanics, like me, work on all parts of a car, while others specialize in one area, such as tires or brakes.

1

At 8:00 a.m., I arrive at the shop and check my appointments for the day. My first customer arrives with her car. The engine has been making a whining sound, and she's asked me to find out what's wrong. I get to work.

2

Using a special lift, I raise the car up so I can look underneath. I remove various parts, clean them, and change the oil. I put everything back together and take the car for a test drive. The whining noise has stopped. I bring the car back, and the customer is very happy, which makes me happy!

3

My next customer arrives for a service. This is a thorough inspection to make sure his truck is in good working order and safe to drive. I check the tires, brakes, oil levels, and that the lights, turn signals, and wipers are working properly. Sometimes repairs can be expensive, so the customer is very relieved to hear that everything is fine!

4

I spend the rest of the day working on more cars and supervising one of the less-experienced mechanics. In this repair shop, the more-experienced mechanics often help newly qualified colleagues improve their skills.

5

Soon it's the end of the day. But my work doesn't stop when I leave the shop! Car technology is changing all the time, so I keep up-to-date with all the latest developments by reading and taking evening classes.

MY JOB: BEST AND WORST PARTS

BEST: I really enjoy the challenge of finding out what's wrong with a car.

WORST: I'm usually covered in oil and grease stains by the end of the day.

POLITICIAN

In my job as a politician, I get to help write the country's laws ... though there's a lot more to it than that! I'm a representative in the House, part of the US Congress. I work closely with my district's (local community) constituents. The voters share their concerns or problems, and I come up with ideas for new legislation to help.

There's no set path to becoming a politician, but it all starts with a passion for helping people. Since high school, I've built up skills and experience through doing lots of different jobs and activities, from being class president and a member of my college debating society, to volunteering for a charity, and working as an aide to a local politician.

1

It's 7:00 a.m., and I'm already working! I'm video calling with a local reporter to talk about a new bill I've proposed. A group of my constituents asked me to take action on the high levels of pollution in our city, and I've spent months preparing a bill that should reduce the impact. Later today, other representatives will vote in Congress to decide if this new bill should become law. It'll be a big moment!

2

After the video call, I drive to my office. Life as a politician is jam-packed—I have meetings all day. Next up is a chat with a group of schoolchildren from my district who have come for a tour and to learn more about politics. I like to meet my constituents face-to-face.

3

At 9:30 a.m., I meet with my campaign manager to talk about my election campaign. Representatives are reelected every two years, and the next election is coming up soon. We're working on a new social media campaign to attract young voters. I need to make sure people of all ages are keen to vote for me.

4

After a few more meetings and a quick lunch break, a group of teachers come to see me. They want to set up an education program that will help more young people to succeed in school and go on to college. The program will include providing tutoring services, advice on college applications, and financial aid. I agree to lend my support—this sounds like a great program.

5

It's almost time for the debate on my bill. I spend some time reading over my notes and practicing. I'm used to speaking in front of lots of people, but it's always important to be prepared. I'm ready to convince Congress to vote for my bill!

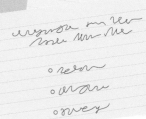

6

At 4:00 p.m., it's showtime. I deliver my speech, then listen as other representatives discuss my proposal. Soon it's time to vote. Using an electronic voting system, representatives vote "Yea" (yes) or "Nay" (no). It's a tense wait for the verdict ...

YEA

NAY

7

The majority of members have voted "Yea." My bill has passed! It will need to be approved by the Senate (the other chamber of Congress) and the president before it becomes law, but it's a great start. I can't wait to tell my constituents!

MY JOB: BEST AND WORST PARTS

BEST: Getting to represent and fight for my constituents is a real honor.

WORST: It's a busy job, so sometimes I have to miss out on spending time with my family.

NURSE

I work in a hospital, where I help deal with a variety of injuries and illnesses. I earned a bachelor's degree in nursing, then took a special exam to become a registered nurse.

Some nurses, *like me, work on general wards, while others specialize in one area, such as geriatrics (older people), cardiac (heart), or pediatrics (children). Whatever area they work in, all nurses need to be compassionate, caring people who love helping others.*

1

I arrive at work at 7:00 a.m. and get changed into my scrubs. I talk with the night shift nurse who is handing over to me. She gives me an update on each patient, so I know what care they will need today.

2

I get started on my morning rounds. Mornings are really busy! I walk around my ward, stopping at each bed to have a chat with the patient and check how they are feeling today. I take their blood pressure, give them their medication, and help them with eating breakfast if needed. I make sure I write down everything in their patient notes.

3

The time passes in a flash, and after lunch, it's the afternoon rounds. I give out more medications and prepare a patient for being discharged. I make sure that she knows how and when to take her medication. Educating patients on their own care is really important to keeping them as safe and healthy as possible.

4

Later, I change a patient's dressing on his infected eye. I talk to him about his treatment plan. He is worried about taking the new medication, but I answer his questions and reassure him that it will make him feel much better.

5

It's nearly the end of my shift. Before I head home, I make sure all the patients' notes are up-to-date, and tell the night shift nurse what's happened today. There's a lot of paperwork in my job, but I don't mind—I love what I do!

MY JOB: BEST AND WORST PARTS

BEST: It makes my day to see patients get better and return home.

WORST: Some days are especially busy, and if we don't have enough staff, it can get very stressful.

MIDWIFE

I love my job as a midwife. I provide health care to women before, during, and after they give birth. Every day is different!

1

Today, I'm working a 12-hour shift. I start by checking on each of the pregnant women in my care. I've been working with them throughout their pregnancies—monitoring their health and giving support and advice—so I'm not a stranger to them. This helps them feel calm and safe, and also means I'm up-to-date with all their needs.

2

One of the women has just arrived on the ward. She is worried because she hasn't felt much movement from the baby today. Using a special machine, I check the baby's heartbeat. It sounds normal, so I reassure the mother-to-be that the baby is safe and well.

I first trained as a nurse, then earned a graduate degree to become a midwife. I work in a hospital, but some midwives visit pregnant women in their own homes. I work a lot with nurses and obstetricians— doctors who specialize in pregnancy, childbirth, and women's health.

3

Next, I'm called to a patient who is ready to give birth. I stay with her and help her, and soon enough a little baby boy is born! After weighing the baby and checking that he is healthy, I return him to his parents so they can get to know each other. I'll come back later to make sure that mother and baby are happy and comfortable.

4

Later, I'm joined by a student midwife who is learning on the job. A patient is feeling unwell, and we need to do a blood test to find out what is wrong. I watch carefully as the student takes the blood—she does great. Helping students and junior teammates is one of my favorite parts of the job.

5

By the end of my shift, I've helped bring four babies into the world! I'm just about to leave when something colorful catches my eye at the nurses' station: it's a thank-you balloon from a family I helped last week!

MY JOB: BEST AND WORST PARTS

BEST: There's nothing better than seeing parents meet their babies.

WORST: Working through the night can be tough!

OCCUPATIONAL THERAPIST

When a person has a developmental disorder, or suffers an injury or illness, this can sometimes make everyday activities harder. It's my job to find ways to help patients adapt, regain their abilities, or teach them to use equipment that will help. I get to work with people of all ages, each with their own story—and I love it!

I studied for several years to become an occupational therapist. I earned a degree in biology in college, followed by a master's degree and passing a special exam. I often work closely with other professionals, such as psychologists (see pages 20–21), doctors (see pages 10–11), physical therapists (see page 47), and speech and language therapists (see page 46). We all share one aim: to help patients live their happiest, healthiest lives.

1

It's 7:00 a.m., and I'm starting my day visiting the home of an older patient. He has recently had a stroke—a condition that means he has lost some of the ability to move one side of his body. He now finds day-to-day tasks, such as washing and dressing, more difficult than before. Today, we are working on ways he can dress himself. With enough time and practice, I'm confident he will be able to manage it again.

2

I take a look around the patient's home. To make daily tasks easier for him, we will install equipment, called aids, around the house. For example, he will need grab rails so he can help himself in and out of the bathtub, and a lowered surface in the kitchen so he can prepare food from his wheelchair. I explain the plans to the patient, and he's so happy. I love helping people gain more independence.

3

Next, I head to the therapy clinic. In my job, I visit patients who can't travel, or when I need to assess a home, but other times patients come to the clinic for their appointments. I enjoy working from the clinic because I get to speak to and share advice with other therapists.

4

At 9:00 a.m., I see a young man who is recovering from a hand injury. This has stopped him from being able to work as a carpenter. We practice some exercises to help build the strength back in his hand, such as picking up coins and putting them in a jar. He's making great progress—if he continues with these exercises every day, he'll be back to work in no time!

5

Next, I see a woman who has arthritis. The painful, swollen joints in her back prevent her from doing many daily tasks. We talk about what activities are important to her. She misses being able to garden the most. I reassure her that with special exercises, she'll be back digging and planting in no time! It's really important to stay positive so our patients continue to do their exercises.

6

After lunch, I work with a child who has cerebral palsy, which is a group of disorders that can cause problems with movement and coordination. We work on her motor skills by doing an ice-cube painting. I ask her to hold the slippery dyed ice cubes and move them over the paper. She has so much fun, and manages to hold the cubes for a significant period of time. I often use arts and crafts like this because if patients enjoy the therapy, they're more likely to try their best.

7

After seeing a few more patients, I spend the rest of the afternoon writing up my notes and checking my schedule for tomorrow. My last task of the day is to call some of my patients' families to keep them in the loop. In some cases, such as where a patient is very elderly, it's important their family knows about their loved one's treatment programs, so they can help them with their exercises or special equipment.

8

Soon it's 5:30 p.m., and time to go home. It's been a successful day; I managed to help all my patients make some progress, so I feel really proud!

MY JOB: BEST AND WORST PARTS

BEST: It's so rewarding helping people get back to enjoying life again.

WORST: It can be challenging to get patients to practice and exercise.

29

POSTAL WORKER

I work for the postal service as a mail carrier, delivering mail to homes and businesses around the city. I became a mail carrier because I enjoy keeping active, being outdoors, and working with people. Sitting in an office all day just wasn't for me! After high school I took a special exam to become a postal worker, and then I learned on the job.

There are lots of other jobs working for the postal service. For example, mail sorters prepare the mail for delivery, while clerks work in post offices, collecting packages, taking money for postage, and selling mailing and packaging supplies.

1

At 7:00 a.m., I arrive at the post office and "clock in." I use a special machine to show what time I arrive and leave.

2

I check what route I'll be taking today and start collecting the mail and packages to be delivered. The mail sorters have already organized the letters into different sections by address. I put the letters into trays in order of the route I'll be following. I load the trays and packages into a cart, and wheel it out to the mail truck.

3

After loading the mail onto the mail truck, I set off on my route. At about 8:00 a.m., I arrive at my first "park point," where I park my truck. Some neighbors wave at me and I wave back. I've done this route many times before, so I'm a familiar face around the community!

4

I fill my satchel with letters and set off on foot: it's quicker and easier than driving from door to door. There's a lot of walking in this job, and that's why I like it! Thankfully, it's warm and sunny today, but even on a cold day, I just make sure to wrap up warm.

5

Once I've delivered all the letters, I return for the packages. If packages are too big or too heavy to carry, I take the truck. Using a special machine, I scan the packages to record that they've been delivered.

DELIVERED

11:50 a.m.

6

I have one more package to deliver. I knock on the door and a little girl answers it with her mom. She's been expecting a package from her pen pal and is really excited to finally receive it! My job helps people from all over the world stay connected like this, and I love it!

7

I've finished one section of the route just in time for lunch. After grabbing a quick sandwich, I continue delivering mail throughout the afternoon. I stop at an office building where I need to deliver mail to a few different businesses that have offices inside. I use a special master key to unlock the right mailboxes.

8

At 4:00 p.m., I return to my truck. All the trays are empty, so my work is done! I drive back to the post office, clock out, and head home, where there's a big pile of mail waiting for me ... it's my birthday!

MY JOB: BEST AND WORST PARTS

BEST: I like making someone's day by delivering the mail they've been waiting for.

WORST: Sometimes overexcited pets can jump up at the mailbox—or the mail carrier!

MEDICAL RESEARCH SCIENTIST

I've always been curious about how things work—especially inside our bodies! I enjoyed science at school, and wanted a job that would help others. As a medical research scientist, I spend lots of my time in a laboratory, looking for ways to improve people's health. I love using science to make a difference.

In my job, I study viruses that infect our bodies and cause diseases. I work to develop new vaccines to fight these viruses and stop us from getting sick. I studied hard to get my job, starting with a bachelor's degree in biology, followed by a master's degree and PhD in virology (the study of viruses), as well as lots of research, training, and work experience.

1

I start off my day at the lab, checking on the results of an overnight experiment. Before I enter, I put on my protective equipment. I sometimes have to deal with harmful chemicals or substances, so I need to make sure I am safe.

2

For my experiment, I am actually growing a virus! Viruses grow by infecting cells inside our bodies, then making copies of themselves. I have mixed a tiny amount of virus together with some human cells. If I can understand how the virus copies itself, this will help me to find a vaccine that stops it from growing.

3

I look at the cells through a microscope—they are too small to see without one. The virus inside the cells hasn't grown as much as I had expected. I will need to spend some time thinking about why this has happened, and what changes I will need to make.

4

It's time to head over to the office. This is where I write reports, check emails, and have meetings with other researchers. But first, I catch up on reading, reviewing scientific news and journal articles. It's really important to stay in touch with what's going on in the world of science. There are new discoveries being made all the time!

5

I get back to thinking about my experiment. I create graphs and make notes about the results. It may be that I didn't use the correct human cells, or perhaps I didn't add the right amount of virus. Being a scientist is like working on a huge jigsaw puzzle: I spend a lot of my time figuring out how one little puzzle piece fits into the bigger picture!

6

I'm concentrating so hard that I barely notice it's lunchtime. I meet some colleagues in the cafeteria for lunch. We usually end up talking about science—it is a passion we all share, after all!

7

I spend the afternoon writing notes for a scientific conference I'll be presenting at next month. Traveling around the world to meet other scientists is one of my favorite parts of the job. We share our research and learn a lot from each other. I can't wait!

MY JOB: BEST AND WORST PARTS

BEST: Every day there's the possibility that I'll find a way to change people's health for the better. There's nothing more exciting than that!

WORST: It can be frustrating when an experiment doesn't work. But I've learned to keep on trying.

8

It's getting late, but I still have some more work to do, so I head back to the lab. I make a change to my experiment, increasing the quantity of the virus. Tomorrow morning I'll be back in the lab again to continue my research. I wonder what I will discover ...

SCHOOL COUNSELOR

As a high school guidance counselor, I help students who may be feeling sad or overwhelmed, are struggling with school, or just need someone to talk to. I listen to their problems and feelings, and talk through solutions that might work for them. I also give advice about colleges and careers. Helping young people feel safe, happy, and excited about their future is what I love to do!

I started out as a teacher, but soon realized I preferred helping students with more than just their academic studies. So, I earned a master's degree in school counseling and took tests to become certified. Now I work with students in a busy high school, helping them deal with all kinds of issues.

1

It's 9:00 a.m., and I'm in the school hallway, greeting students as they arrive. I notice a student in tears, and I invite her to come to my office for a chat. She's had a fight with some friends, so we talk about ways she can move forward, and she soon feels a bit better. Sometimes just talking can help.

2

I head to a classroom for a guidance session about mental health. I often give these sessions to help students look after their well-being, from getting regular exercise and eating right to getting enough sleep. One student says that he's been going to bed earlier than usual and he feels much happier. It's great to know my advice is making a difference!

3

After the session, I go back to my office and see students one-on-one for the rest of the morning. One student is worried he doesn't have good enough grades for college. We take a look at his recent reports. It's clear he's been working hard, and his grades are on track, so I reassure him and remind him not to put too much pressure on himself.

4

At lunchtime, I run a college prep club. I regularly advise students individually about college and careers, but this club is an informal chance to talk about different colleges, what to expect, how to apply, and so on. I make sure I have lots of college brochures to share.

5

After seeing more students in the afternoon, it's the end of the school day. I stay on to call or write to parents about any problems they need to know about. Finally, I cycle home and make sure to eat a healthy meal—after all, I have to practice what I teach!

MY JOB: BEST AND WORST PARTS

BEST: I love helping students learn the skills they need for a successful future.

WORST: It's sad when students don't put in the effort and end up missing out.

HUMAN RESOURCES MANAGER

All businesses, from small dental practices to hotels and hospitals, have one thing in common: they need good people to work for them. That's where I come in! I hire people to work for my company, organize staff training, and make sure that this is a happy and safe place to work.

I've always wanted to work with people, so I went to college and earned a degree in human resources management. I started out as an assistant and worked my way up to manager at a children's clothing company.

1
When I get to work, I make sure I say a friendly "hello" to any colleagues I pass on the way to my office. It's important that they know who I am so that they can reach out to me if they have any problems or questions.

2
This morning, the sales manager and I are interviewing candidates to join the sales team. We're looking for someone who will fit in well and is passionate about our company. I ask questions and make notes on each candidate. After the interviews, we agree on the best person for the job, and I can't wait to break the good news to her later!

4
Later, I meet with a staff member who has been off work with a back injury. We talk about how we can make his work space more comfortable. I order him a special desk chair that will support his back better. It's my job to solve problems and to make sure our staff stay happy and healthy while working for us.

3
After lunch, it's time for some staff training. I organize these sessions often because it's important for staff to have the chance to develop new skills. Today, the session is about public speaking. I make sure the expert trainer is all set up, and I stay throughout to help.

MY JOB: BEST AND WORST PARTS

BEST: I relish putting my mind to solving problems.

WORST: Dealing with conflict can be stressful.

5
Usually I finish work at 5:00 p.m., but tonight a staff member is retiring. We gather to thank her for all her hard work over the years, and to enjoy a slice of cake ... or two!

35

911 DISPATCHER

When someone dials 911 in an emergency, I'm the person on the other end of the line. I gather all the information from the caller and pass it on to the correct emergency unit (police, fire, or medical) so help can be sent right away.

2

I take my first call: a woman is in a panic, saying that her car has just caught fire. Safety always comes first! I make sure she's a safe distance from the car before asking questions to find out her location, name, and what exactly has happened. I enter all the details into our computer system and alert the fire services through the radio. I reassure the caller that help is on the way.

To get my job, I had to complete a training program, pass a test, and learn basic first aid. I then trained on the job, learning to use the computer and radio systems. Staying calm and patient and having great communication skills are key in this job.

1

At 6:00 a.m., I arrive for my shift at the dispatch center. I take a seat, put on my headset, and get ready to start taking calls. I never know what kinds of calls, or how many calls I will receive—every day is different.

3

Time for a deep breath. What a start to my day! My next call is from a grocery store manager who reports that a robbery has just taken place. I take all the information I need from him. He is very upset, but I reassure him that the police are on their way and will do what they can.

4

Time to take another call. An older man says his wife has slipped and fallen. I direct him to talk to his wife and ask specific questions to find out more about her potential injuries. I keep him on the phone until the ambulance arrives, helping him and his wife to stay calm.

MY JOB: BEST AND WORST PARTS

BEST: I get to help my community in lots of different ways.

WORST: Listening to people's worst moments can be really hard.

5

I continue to take calls for the rest of my shift, until 6:00 p.m. There are burglaries, a flooded road, and a traffic accident, to name a few! Being a dispatcher is a busy job and can be stressful at times, but it's all worth it to help keep people safe.

PARAMEDIC

When a person suddenly becomes sick or injured, paramedics are one of the first to arrive on scene. We treat the patient, then transport them to the hospital. As a paramedic, I often give medications, treat wounds, do CPR, and more! I'm passionate about giving the best care I can to people who are in need.

I studied and trained for a few years, and had to pass exams to become certified. Today, I work for a hospital in the emergency department. Other paramedics work on helicopters, in fire stations, or even on cruise ships!

1

I start my shift at 7:00 a.m. My partner and I inspect our ambulance and equipment. We need to make sure we have everything we need. We also check that the lights and siren are working before we turn on our radio and wait for the first call of the day.

2

Our first call comes in from dispatch. A 68-year-old man is suffering chest pains. This could be life-threatening, so we mustn't waste any time. Sirens on, we race to the patient's home. As paramedics we're trained to drive at high speeds, but we always make sure to stay safe.

3

When we reach the patient, I run some tests and suspect he is having a heart attack. I give him medication right away, then my partner helps me move him into the ambulance. My partner drives while I stay in the back with the patient and look after him. At the hospital, I'll let the staff know his symptoms and what treatment we've given him before we leave him in their care.

4

Once we're back in the ambulance, we don't have to wait long for the next call. A teenage girl has injured her leg playing soccer. We hurry to the park as quickly as possible. I check the patient and realize she likely has a fracture, so we splint her leg and take her to the hospital.

MY JOB: BEST AND WORST PARTS

BEST: I get to help people every day, saving lives and making a difference.

WORST: Sometimes an injury is too serious and the only thing I can do to help is drive as fast as possible to the hospital.

5

The day flies by with many more calls and trips to and from the hospital. I even help a woman deliver a baby! It's been an action-packed day. I unwind with a good movie at home—an action movie, of course!

LAWYER

I enjoy a good argument: that's why I love being a lawyer! There are different types of lawyers, such as those who deal with businesses, or those who work with families. As a prosecutor, I represent the people of the state, prosecuting offenders. In my job, I need excellent speaking, writing, reading, and debating skills.

1

It's 9:00 a.m., and I'm in the office, preparing paperwork. I'll be spending the morning in court, prosecuting a burglary case. I must make sure I have all the evidence ready to present to the judge and the jury. They will be the ones to make the decisions about the case.

You have to be dedicated to be a lawyer, since there's lots of studying to do to get there! First, I earned a bachelor's degree, then I graduated from law school, and passed the bar exam to become fully qualified. Today, I work with other lawyers as well as police officers (see pages 12–13) and forensic scientists, who uncover scientific evidence, such as fingerprints.

2

At 10:00 a.m., I get to court and meet with the woman whose house was burgled. She is still very upset, but I reassure her that I'll do my very best to bring the burglar to justice and keep her neighborhood safe.

3

We are called into the courtroom. The defendant (the person accused of committing the crime) is there with his lawyer. I stand up in front of the judge and jury and explain that I have strong evidence to prove that the man is guilty: his fingerprints were found on the window of the house. There is also a witness: someone who saw him leave the victim's house.

4

The witness arrives to give evidence. He takes his place on the witness stand, and I ask him questions: What time was he at the scene? What exactly did he see? The jury needs as many facts as possible to help them decide if the defendant is guilty or innocent, and it's my job to get them those facts.

5

The defense lawyer then cross-examines the witness. She wants to try to prove that the defendant didn't commit the crime. It's important for the jury to hear both sides of the story, so they can come to a fair decision.

6

Once all the evidence from both sides is presented, and all the witnesses are questioned, it's time to sum up the case. I love this part—it's all about making a good argument and convincing the jury. Afterward, we await the verdict. The jury finds the defendant guilty. We've won the case! The judge will decide on the sentence. Hopefully, after this, the burglar will choose to stay on the right side of the law.

7

After a successful morning, I spend the afternoon preparing for tomorrow's court cases. One is about an act of vandalism on someone's car. I gather all the evidence, including pictures of the damaged car and CCTV footage. I also call the witnesses to confirm that they will be in court to give evidence tomorrow.

8

There's a lot to get through, so I work later than usual. Being a lawyer can be hard work, but I don't mind! If it means I see justice being done, then it's all worth it. I go home, but my arguing doesn't stop for the day—at dinner I have a debate with my daughter who thinks we should get a pet dog. Let's see if she can convince me!

MY JOB: BEST AND WORST PARTS

BEST: I get to help make my community a safer, fairer place.

WORST: It's frustrating when I lose a case.

PHARMACIST

I'm fascinated by medicine and I'm good with people—that's why I became a community pharmacist. I run my own pharmacy, providing the local people with the medicines they need. It's my job to dispense medication, advise customers about taking it, and offer general health advice. Helping people stay healthy and happy is what my job is all about.

A love of learning is important in my job. I had to earn a Doctor of Pharmacy degree and pass an exam to get my license, and I keep my knowledge current, with continuing education classes. Most pharmacists work as either hospital or community pharmacists (like me). But some work in other settings, such as nursing homes, health clinics, or laboratories.

1

I arrive at the pharmacy at 8:30 a.m., and I start preparing prescriptions. A prescription is a written direction from a doctor saying what medication a patient needs to take. Patients bring or send the prescriptions to the pharmacy, and I dispense the medication, ready for them to pick up and take home.

2

I carefully measure out the medicines according to each prescription. I need to have really good attention to detail. A patient can react badly even to the tiniest difference in dosage. Their safety is in my hands!

3

At 9:00 a.m., it's time to open the doors. A young man arrives to pick up his medication. He asks me lots of questions: How often should he take it? Will it cause any side effects? Is it safe? I've already researched the medication, so I'm able to answer his questions and reassure him.

4

In the afternoon, a woman comes in asking for painkillers for her bad back. I find out she's taking other medication which means most painkillers aren't safe for her. I help her find some pills that she can take without needing a prescription, and she thanks me for my advice. Being kind and good at listening are really important qualities for a pharmacist.

MY JOB: BEST AND WORST PARTS

BEST: I love getting to know my customers—some have been coming to my pharmacy for years!

WORST: Sometimes people can be challenging to deal with, but it's often because they are unwell or worried.

5

I spend the rest of the day helping customers and placing orders for the medicines that are running low, then I close the store. On my way home, I drop off a prescription for an older man who is too frail to pick it up himself. He's so thankful, it makes my day!

DENTIST

Unlike some people, I've always enjoyed visiting the dentist. Growing up, my dentist was kind and funny, and the equipment she used looked really cool! I studied biology in college, then I went to dental school for another four years. Today, I work in a small practice.

I'm a general dentist and I spend most days doing checkups, fillings, or removing teeth. Sometimes, people need more specialized treatment. For example, an endodontist treats the soft tissues and nerves inside the tooth, while orthodontists specialize in fixing crooked or crowded teeth.

1

I start the day with a staff meeting, involving the dentists, dental assistants, and dental hygienists at the practice. We discuss today's patients and their treatments.

2

My first patient is a woman who has a cavity in one of her teeth and needs a filling. She's a little nervous. While the dental assistant prepares the equipment, I chat with the patient, and try to put her at ease. It doesn't take long to put the filling in place, and once it's over the patient is surprised by how quick and pain-free it was.

3

My next patient is a man who has a painful tooth. I take an X-ray which shows that the tooth is damaged. It will need a protective cover called a crown. The crown needs to be custom-made to fit over his tooth, so I take impressions and put a temporary crown in place. He will need to return for another appointment to have the permanent crown put in.

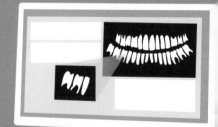

4

Next, I see a girl who is here for a general checkup. I notice that her teeth are quite crowded, which could cause problems when she's older, so I refer her to an orthodontist. She may need to have braces to move her teeth to a better position.

5

My last appointment is a mother and her little boy. He's very excited to be sitting in the big chair! I check his teeth and make sure he knows how to brush them properly. And then for my favorite part—giving him a sticker for being so brave!

MY JOB: BEST AND WORST PARTS

BEST: Dentistry is exciting: there are always new developments to keep up with, from smart toothbrushes to robotic dentists!

WORST: It's a shame when people miss appointments because of nerves—one of the best ways to avoid needing dental work is to visit the dentist regularly.

FIREFIGHTER

Being a firefighter is exciting—no two days are ever the same! But there is a lot more to the job than putting out fires. Firefighters handle all kinds of emergencies, from medical crises to floods. We rescue and treat injured people, and educate our community about fire safety. We need to be hardworking and brave, and have a real wish to help others.

I always wanted to be a firefighter. After high school, I went to a fire academy to learn firefighting, rescue, and lifesaving skills, then passed a lot of tests before joining my local fire department. If I keep learning and working hard, maybe one day I can become the fire chief.

1

It's 7:00 a.m., and I'm at the fire station, ready for my 24-hour shift. We could get an emergency call at any time, so I need to be prepared. I grab my safety gear and place it by the fire truck. I check that my air tank is full and that our truck and equipment are in perfect working order. We're good to go!

2

At 8:30 a.m., I'm ready for breakfast! I eat and chat with my colleagues in the fire station kitchen. It's really important that we all get along: during emergencies, we need to rely on each other and work as a team.

3

After breakfast, we do training exercises. We're always working hard to improve our firefighting skills. Today, we use special tools to practice removing a car door, for when someone is trapped inside.

4

Next, a group of schoolchildren arrive for a tour of the fire station. I talk to them about fire prevention and safety, as well as teach them how to save a life using CPR. We finish up with the most fun part: exploring the fire truck!

5

At 12:00 p.m., it's time for lunch. Suddenly, the alarm sounds. We rush to the fire truck and put on our gear. The 911 dispatcher (see page 36) informs us of a house fire. We jump in the truck, sirens on, and drive to the scene.

6

The captain gives us our instructions. First, we must make sure everyone is safe. The homeowners are outside, but one of them has a burn on his arm. Firefighters are trained to give emergency medical care, so one of my colleagues treats the wound until the ambulance arrives. The rest of us hook up the hose to the truck and tackle the fire. It doesn't take long to get the flames under control. We all breathe a sigh of relief! After cleaning up the scene, we head back to the station.

7

Back at the station, we clean the fire truck and check all our equipment again, making sure everything is ready for the next emergency. Next up, it's over to the gym for a workout. Being a firefighter is a tough, physical job, so we work hard to stay healthy and strong.

8

After dinner, we do chores. The fire station is like our second home. When we're working a shift, we eat and sleep here, so we take turns with the housekeeping. Soon, I'm tired out, so I head to the sleeping quarters to get some rest. But I know that another call could come at any moment ...

9

Sure enough, at midnight, the alarm sounds. There's been a vehicle crash! Luckily, the drivers are unharmed, but one of them is trapped in her car. Time to put our training into action!

MY JOB: BEST AND WORST PARTS

BEST: I love being part of a team that helps people, and I also like that it's such an active, physical job.

WORST: There's always a risk that someone on my team could be injured on the job.

YOUR PERFECT JOB MATCH

With so many jobs out there, it can be tricky to choose between them. Use this guide to find out which careers match up with your skills, personal qualities, and interests.

Doctor

Nurse

Special education teacher

Lawyer

Politician

Paramedic

Public speaking

Psychologist

Dentist

Good at science

If you have good communication skills, these jobs might interest you.

Development director

Pharmacist

Medical research scientist

These jobs are for people who find science fascinating.

WHAT ARE YOUR SKILLS?

School counselor

Psychologist

Occupational therapist

Good at listening

Doctor

Development director

Understanding others is a key skill in these jobs.

Social worker

Daycare center manager

Mechanic

Organized

Special education teacher

Some careers need people who are good at making plans.

Refuse collector

Practical

Bus driver

Human resources manager

These jobs are ideal for those who like to be hands-on.

Shipping clerk

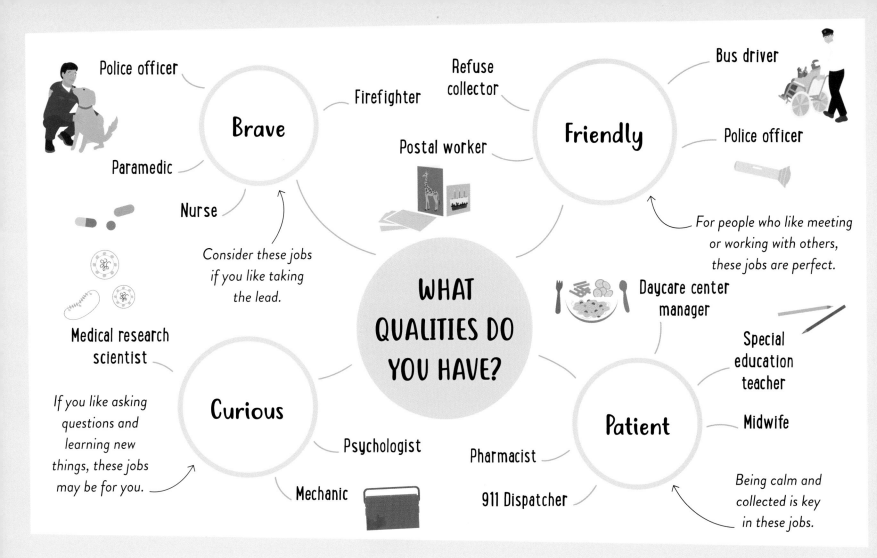

WHAT QUALITIES DO YOU HAVE?

Brave
- Police officer
- Paramedic
- Nurse
- Firefighter

Consider these jobs if you like taking the lead.

Friendly
- Refuse collector
- Postal worker
- Bus driver
- Police officer

For people who like meeting or working with others, these jobs are perfect.

Curious
- Medical research scientist
- Psychologist
- Mechanic

If you like asking questions and learning new things, these jobs may be for you.

Patient
- Daycare center manager
- Special education teacher
- Midwife
- Pharmacist
- 911 Dispatcher

Being calm and collected is key in these jobs.

WHAT ARE YOUR INTERESTS AND GOALS?

Helping people feel better
- Occupational therapist
- Doctor
- Pharmacist
- Nurse
- Dentist

If you enjoy caring for others, you'll like these jobs.

Keeping people safe
- Police officer
- Paramedic
- Firefighter
- 911 Dispatcher

These are the jobs for you if you thrive under pressure and want to protect others.

Making the world a better place
- Medical research scientist
- Refuse collector
- Politician
- Development director

You need to be motivated and interested in helping to create a brighter future to do well in these jobs.

THERE'S MORE ...

You've read about a lot of jobs that involve helping people in this book, but there are many more to choose from. Some of these were mentioned very briefly in the book and others will be completely new to you.

TRANSLATOR/INTERPRETER

For those who love learning languages and helping people communicate, this could be the perfect job! Translators translate written text, for example, novels or scientific reports, from one language to another. Interpreters translate the spoken word as it's happening: they listen to the speaker and translate what they are saying so that people around them can understand. It's important to have really good language and listening skills for these jobs.

SPEECH AND LANGUAGE THERAPIST

A speech and language therapist works with people of all ages who have difficulties speaking and communicating, or eating and swallowing. Whether it's helping an injured patient talk again, or a baby with a feeding problem, these therapists can make a real difference to people's lives. Being caring and patient are important qualities for this job.

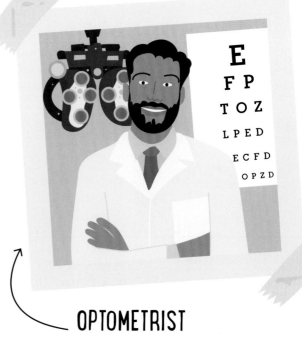

OPTOMETRIST

Optometrists are eye doctors who specialize in primary health care for the eyes. They examine patients' eyes to check for vision problems or diseases, and prescribe and fit glasses and contact lenses. Optometrists need to have a good attention to detail, and since they use precise tools for examining and treating patients' eyes, a steady hand is useful, too!

NURSING HOME MANAGER

A nursing home manager is in charge of the day-to-day running of a nursing home, making sure that its elderly residents are safe and well taken care of. It's the perfect job for someone who is kind and sensitive, and who wants to help older people lead happy, comfortable lives. Being a good leader is important in this job, too, since nursing home managers are responsible for leading a team of workers.

HANDYMAN

A handyman carries out small jobs, usually around people's homes. They might put up shelves, do painting and decorating, repair broken furniture, or help with gardening. They need to work well with their hands, and be able to use tools, from drills to paint rollers. It also helps to be strong and fit because they often need to carry heavy items or climb up and down ladders—sometimes at the same time!

PHYSICAL THERAPIST

When someone is recovering from an injury or illness, they may still have physical problems, such as back pain or difficulty walking. A physical therapist works with patients to ease their pain and help them recover more quickly. They use their in-depth knowledge of the human body to offer suitable treatment including muscle-strengthening exercises, massage, and stretches.

GROCERY STORE CLERK

For anyone who sees themselves as helpful, friendly, and organized, working in a grocery store could be just for them! A grocery store clerk helps with the smooth running of a grocery store. They might stock shelves, receive orders, or work the cash register. Most importantly, they need to enjoy being around people, as they'll be greeting customers, answering questions, and helping them with their shopping.

First American Edition 2021
Kane Miller, A Division of EDC Publishing

Copyright © 2021 Quarto Publishing plc

Published by arrangement with Ivy Kids, an imprint of The Quarto Group.
All rights reserved. No part of this book may be reproduced, transmitted
or stored in an information retrieval system in any form or by any means, graphic,
electronic or mechanical, including photocopying, taping and recording,
without prior written permission from the publisher.

For information contact:
Kane Miller, A Division of EDC Publishing
5402 S 122nd E Ave, Tulsa, OK 74146
www.kanemiller.com
www.myubam.com

Library of Congress Control Number: 2021930477

Manufactured in Guangdong, China CC072021

ISBN: 978-1-68464-280-9

1 2 3 4 5 6 7 8 9 10

MIX
Paper from
responsible sources
FSC
www.fsc.org
FSC® C008047